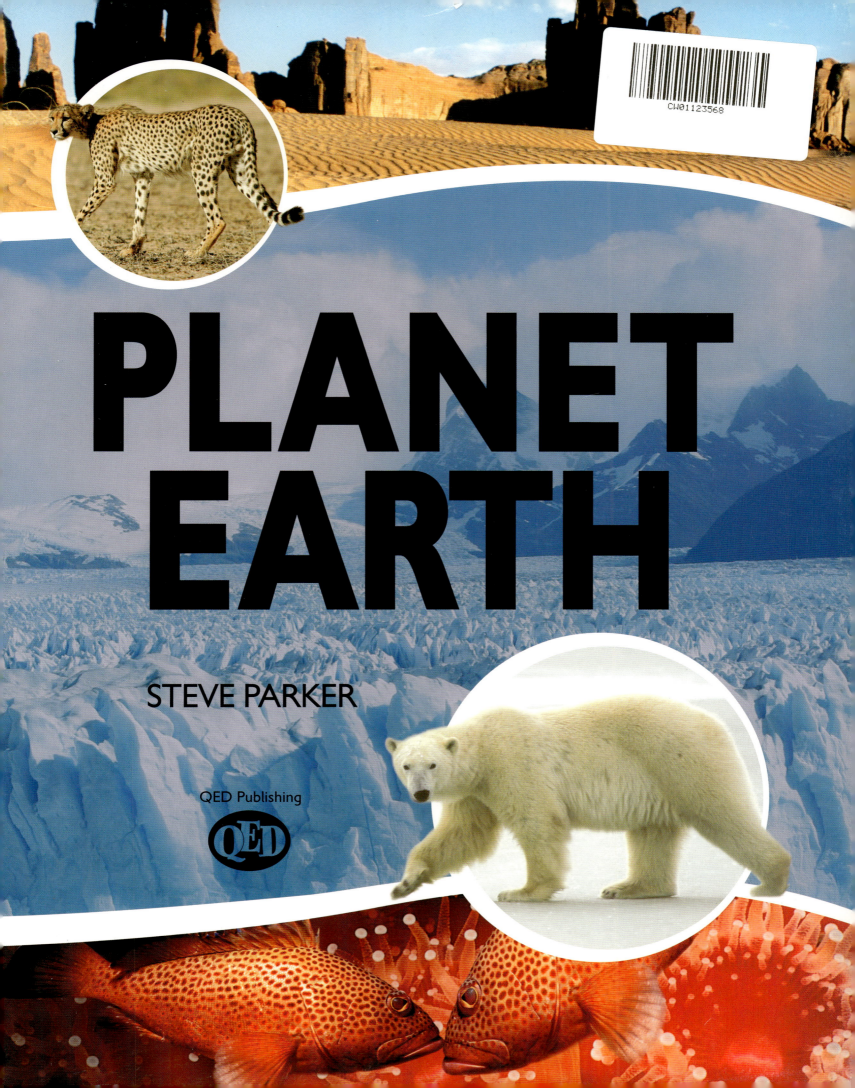

PLANET EARTH

STEVE PARKER

QED Publishing

QED

First published in the UK in 2010 by
QED Publishing
A Quarto Group company
226 City Road
London EC1V 2TT

www.qed-publishing.co.uk

A catalogue record for this book is available from the British Library.

ISBN 978 1 84835 277 3

Author Steve Parker
Design and Editorial East River Partnership

Publisher Steve Evans
Creative Director Zeta Davies
Managing Editor Amanda Askew

Printed and bound in China

Picture credits
(t=top, b=bottom, l=left, c=centre, fc=front cover)
Corbis 15 George H H Huey, 17 Peter Johnson, 29 Brian A Vikander, 77t Bettmann, 82–83, 83b Tim Davis, 83t Rick Price, 86–87 Reuters, 87r Karen Kasmauski, 110–111 Chris McLaughlin, 111b Ralph White, 113t Jeremy Horner, 114–115 Reuters

Getty Images 9t Chris Sattlberger, 10–11t Jeff Foott, 12–13 Peter Pearson, 13t Paul Chesley, 14 Karen Kasmauski, 15t Time & Life Pictures/Getty Images, 16–117t Lee Frost, 18–19 Gerd Ludwig, 22tl Michael & Patricia Fogden, 31 Bernard van Dierendonck, 34–35b Mattius Klum/National Geographic/ 35b Maria Stenzel/ 38 Tom Till/ 40 Michael & Patricia Fogden/41, 43 Pete Oxford/ 44t Timothy Laman/ 46–47 Norbert Wu/ 49b DEA/R Sacco/ 50 Art Wolfe/ 55 Tui De Roy, 64 Tom Vezo, 64t Jeff Harbers, 69t Jorn Georg Tomter, 70–71t Daniel J Cox, 72t Brian J Skerry, 73t, 74–75, 79 Flip Nicklin, 78–79 Tui De Roy, 79t Bill Curtsinger, 85 Stuart Westmorland, 103t, 109t Norbert Wu, 111t Peter David

NHPA 22 A N T Photo Library, 23 Anthony Bannister, 23t Martin Harvey, 24–25 Martin Harvey, 24t James Carmichael Jr, 24b A N T Photo Library, 42t Nick Garbutt/ 44 Stephen Dalton/ 45r, 53t, 58–59b Martin Harvey/ 48–49t John Shaw/ 57 Nigel J Dennis/ 58–59t Martin Wendler, 63, 81b, 85t Bryan & Cherry Alexander, 91t A N T Photo Library, 92, 92–93 Ernie Janes, 95t Nigel J Dennis, 96t Roger Tidman, 97 Anthony Bannister, 100b Trevor McDonald, 101b Roy Waller, 102b B Jones & M Shimlock, 104–105 A N T Photo Library, 106b M I Walker, 107 Gerard Lacz, 108t Kevin Schafer

Photolibrary 27t, 28–29 Gerald Hinde, 72–73 Doug Perrine, 76 David B Fleetham, 78t Roland Birke, 79t James Watt, 80–81 Kevin Schafer, 84–85 Doug Allen, 108–109 Kevin Schafer, 104 David B Fleetham, 107t James Watt, 106t Roland Birke, 100–101 Doug Perrine

Photoshot 18 Phillip Roullard, 68–69 Fergus Gill

Shutterstock 6c Louise Cukrov, 6–7 Amir Hossein Biparva, 7t Alexey Goosev, 7 Vova Pomortzeff, 8–9 Stasys Eidiejus, 10 Ke Wang, 10–11b Angel's Gate Inc, 12b Kaspars Grinvalds, 14–15b Daryl Faust, 16–17b Jo Ann Snover, 18t Ashley Whitworth, 19b Ronald Sherwood, 20 Dmytro Korolov, 21b Steve Lovegrove, 21 Hagit Berkovich, 25b David Nagy, 26–27 Johan Swanepoel, 29t Johan Swanepoel, 30–31 Stephen Coburn, 38b John Bell/ 46t Snowleopard1/ 34–35t Joe Gough/ 35t EcoPrint/ 37t Jennifer Stone/ 38b Olga Shelego/ 39 Suzanne Long/ 41t Leo/ 42b jaana piira/ 46b Luis Louro/ 47t Timothy Craig Lubcke/ 48–49b Sergey I/ 49t chai kian shin/ 50b Michael Shake/ 51t Karel Gallas/ 51 Alvaro Pantoja/ 52l Peter Graham/ 52t Vova Pomortzeff/ 52 Galyna Andrushko/ 54 Donald Gargano/ 55b fenghui/ 56 Jim Lipschutz/ 57 Patsy A Jacks/ 58l Simone van den Berg/ 59r Grigory Kubatyan, 66t James R Hearn, 74t Halldor Eiriksson, 62b Stasys Eidiejus, 62–63, 80t Jan Martin Will, 64–65, 77b, 80–81 Armin Rose, 66b Andreas Gradin, 66–67 TTphoto, 67t Roman Krochuk, 68t Naturablichter, 69b, 71t, 71b Gail Johnson, 70–71b Sam Chadwick, 72–73 Edward Chin, 76–77 Vera Bogaerts, 86–87t Steve Estvanik, 90 Eric Gevaert, 90–91 Wolfgang Amri, 91b Khlobystov Alexey, 93r Lagui, 94–95 David Mail, 94l Susan flashman, 95b Marco Alegria, 96 Pichugin Dmitry, 97t Carsten Medom Madsen, 98 Jerome Whittingham, 99t Holger W, 100–101 Stuart Elflett, 101t Giuseppe Nocera, 103b Bill Kennedy, 102–103 Elisei Shafer, 105r Vling, 112 Mark Bond, 112–113 Elena Yakusheva, 113 Sapsiwai, 115 Juha Sompinmäki, 115c Mark Yuill

Words in **bold** are explained in the glossary on page 116.

Contents

Deserts

The **driest** lands

Deserts can be sandy, rocky or covered with pebbles. They can be scorching hot or freezing cold, but all deserts are dry.

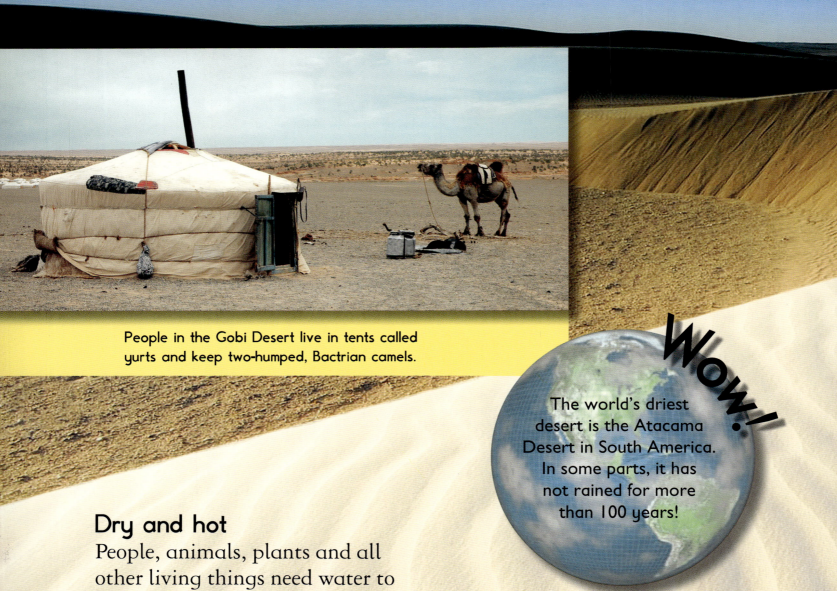

People in the Gobi Desert live in tents called yurts and keep two-humped, Bactrian camels.

Wow!

The world's driest desert is the Atacama Desert in South America. In some parts, it has not rained for more than 100 years!

Dry and hot

People, animals, plants and all other living things need water to survive. Deserts have much less water than forests or grasslands. This is because it hardly ever rains in a desert. If it does rain, the water usually dries in the hot sun, trickles through the thin soil or flows away over bare rock. This is why many deserts appear to have so little life.

The dorcas gazelle digs for plant bulbs in the desert.

It's so... dry!

In a typical desert, if you collected all the rain that fell in a year it would amount to less than 25 centimetres. That is almost three times less rain than in London, England, and four times less than in New York City, USA.

A large area of windswept sand in a desert is known as an erg.

Saving water

About one-quarter of the world's land area is either very dry or true desert. Yet even though these places are so dry, or **arid**, some plants and animals can survive there. These desert creatures and plants have special ways of saving what little water there is. Humans have lived in deserts for thousands of years, too. These people have a different way of life from those living in a town or city. You cannot simply turn on a tap!

Where are deserts?

Most of the large deserts are found towards the middle of the world. They lie above and below the line called the equator.

Great Basin

NORTH AMERICA

Mojave

Sonoran

Chihuahua

Wow!

The Sahara Desert is about the same size as the USA, and much bigger than Australia!

Sahara

North of the equator

Many of the world's largest deserts lie north of the **equator**. One reason for this is that there is more land to the north of the equator than there is to the south. The northern deserts include the Sonoran Desert in North America, the Sahara Desert in North Africa, the Arabian Desert of the Middle East and the Takla Makan and Gobi Deserts in Asia.

SOUTH AMERICA

Sechura

Atacama

Monte
Patagonian

It's so big!

The Sahara Desert is four times bigger than the Arabian Desert, the world's second-largest desert. It is six times bigger than the third-largest desert, the Gobi Desert.

Largest desert

The Sahara Desert, which occupies 9,000,000 square kilometres, is the world's largest desert. It is about 5000 kilometres across. This is almost the same distance as that between London and New York.

In the middle of Australia, the desert stretches as far as you see.

Kara Kum

Gobi

Takla Makan

Turkestan

Thar

CHINA

Arabian

INDIA

Somali

Equator

AFRICA

South of the equator

South of the equator, both Africa and South America have deserts. These are mainly in the south-west of each **continent**. North America has deserts in its south-west, too. The place with the most deserts compared to its size is Australia. More than two-thirds of this huge country is dry land or desert.

Kalahari

amib

Great Sandy

Gibson   Simpson

Great Victoria

AUSTRALIA

The largest southern dry areas are in Australia.

Antarctic

How deserts are formed

Deserts form in places where there are few rain clouds. These can be inland, along dry coasts, and in areas shielded from rain by mountains.

Around the South Pole lies frozen Antarctica. Here, it is too cold to rain.

Continental deserts

The way the Earth spins around and how it is warmed by the Sun affects where winds blow and how clouds form. Often, there are clouds and rain near sea coasts. Farther inland, it is drier. The largest deserts, such as the Sahara, Gobi and Australian deserts, are far from the sea. These are called continental deserts.

Rain falls on mountains around the Mojave Desert, not in the desert itself.

Rain-shadow deserts

Some deserts, such as the Mojave Desert in the United States, are known as rain-shadow deserts. When warm, moist air blows against mountains, it rises and becomes cooler. As it cools, the moisture in the air turns into water drops, which form clouds. As the air moves up the mountains, it loses more and more water as rain or snow. By the time the air reaches the other side of the mountains, it is dry and without clouds. Here, a rain-shadow desert forms.

Coastal deserts

Deserts are found along coasts where the winds are very dry. The Namib in south-west Africa and the Atacama in western South America are both coastal deserts.

Southern Africa's Namib Desert lies beside the cold Atlantic ocean.

11

Types of deserts

Many people imagine that deserts are made up of huge sand dunes. In fact, only about one-fifth of the world's desert areas are sandy.

Hard rock

The type of desert that forms depends on how much sun, wind and rain there is, and also on the type of rock in the ground. Very hard rocks do not break easily, even when the Sun makes them too hot to touch. So the desert is hard and bare.

Uluru, or Ayers Rock, is found in central Australia's desert area. It is the world's largest rock.

Grains of sand

Softer rocks crack as they get warm in the Sun and then go cold at night. They break into small, pebble-sized lumps, then into smaller pieces, which the wind blows around. Gradually, they turn into tiny bits of rock called sand grains.

In Australia, desert rocks and pebbles are known as gibbers.

Curved sand dunes formed by desert winds are known as barchan dunes.

Sand dunes

In sandy deserts, the wind blows loose sand into hills called dunes. These dunes can take different shapes, such as waves, curves or stars, depending on the wind's direction and speed.

It's so... hot 'n' cold!

The Gobi Desert can be 40ºC by day then minus 10ºC at night. Nowhere else is it so hot, then so cold, all in just a few hours.

Desert winds and storms

The weather in a desert is usually hot and dry, but sometimes, a huge storm can blow up. Then, almost anything can happen!

It's so... dusty!
Winds spread up to 200 million tonnes of dust from the Sahara Desert around the world every year. This is known as 'mineral dust' because it contains many **minerals**.

People have to wrap up well to protect themselves during desert sandstorms.

Desert storms

A storm's strong winds swirl around desert sand, forcing people and animals to take cover. Over a long period of time, these sandstorms rub and scrape rocks into strange shapes, such as arches and mushrooms. This process is called **erosion**, and the worn-off bits of rock gradually become new sand grains.

Wow!

The surface of the Black Rock Desert in the United States was smooth enough for Thrust SSC to break the land-speed record with a speed of 1228 kilometres per hour!

Supersonic car Thrust SSC breaking the land-speed record in 1997.

A flash flood hits the desert in Utah's Valley of the Gods in south-west North America.

Flash floods

During a desert thunderstorm, lightning flashes, thunder booms and rain pours down. Water surges into once-dry channels, creating an instant river. This is known as a flash flood. It washes away soil, plants and animals. Yet in a few days, the desert is dry again. In some deserts, the drying water leaves flat, pale, glistening layers of salt. In deserts in the United States, these salt flats are called playas.

Sand blown by the wind in desert areas can sometimes form rocky arches.

Desert plants

Plants in deserts have a difficult time. They must collect as much water as they can, cope with a scorching sun and fight off hungry, plant-eating creatures.

Deep roots

Plants soak up water through their roots. Some desert plants have roots that go down very deep, sometimes ten metres or more. This is as deep as five people standing on top of each other. Other plants have roots that spread out widely. This helps them take in lots of water quickly when it rains.

The saguaro cactus of south-west North America can grow to be more than 15 metres high.

Plant protection

Desert animals eat as many soft plants and leaves as they can find. This is why cacti, acacias and thornbushes have spines, prickles or thorns. They protect these plants from being eaten.

Only giraffes can eat Camel thorn trees. They are tall enough to reach the young, soft leaves at the top.

Wow!

A side branch of the huge saguaro cactus can take more than 75 years to grow!

The welwitschia soaks up water from night-time dew.

Storing water

Some desert plants, such as the cactus, store water in their thick stems. The baobab tree of Africa holds water in its wide trunk. Other desert trees that store water include the quiver tree and Joshua tree in North America, the rare ghaf tree in the Middle East and Asia, and the gum trees of Australia.

It's so... weird!

The welwitschia of the Namib Desert is an unusual plant. It has only two leaves, which grow to be four metres in length and become torn and ragged. This plant lives for more than 1000 years!

Flowers in the desert

After rainfall, the desert suddenly comes alive as flowers grow quickly and make a carpet of colour.

Desert flowers

Where do bright desert flowers suddenly appear from? They start as seeds that may have been lying for many years in sand, soil or cracks in rocks. Rain makes the seeds grow, or **germinate**, into small plants whose flowers quickly open their colourful petals. Desert flowers include the orange-red desert paintbrush flower and the blood-red Sturt's desert pea.

It's so... pesky!

The North African yellow-flowered Sahara mustard plant has spread to deserts in North America. Here, it smothers all the **native** plants!

Producing seeds

When they bloom, desert flowers receive busy visitors, such as bees, flies, beetles and butterflies. These insects hatch from eggs after the rain. They carry dust-like **pollen** from one flower to another so that flowers can make their seeds. In a few weeks, the seeds fall to the ground, where they may lie for a long time. The plants then wither and die, and the desert starts to look bare again.

Spring flowers bloom quickly in North America's Mojave Desert.

Wow!

The vansumberuu flower of the Gobi Desert is so special that people travel for days to pray to it.

Queen butterflies feed on the sweet, sticky nectar of desert flowers.

Animals of the desert

Desert animals have to take in water to survive. Yet some of them never drink!

The one-humped dromedary camels of Africa and Arabia also live wild in Australia.

It's so... thirsty!

A camel can go for two weeks without water. Then, in a few minutes, it can drink more than 100 litres. This is enough water to fill a bath!

Dry droppings

Many desert animals are able to live solely on the water they get from eating fruits and bugs. They do not need to drink extra water. Also, these animals do not lose water from their bodies. They do not **sweat** much, they produce only small amounts of **urine** and their droppings are fairly dry.

Wandering around

Ants and termites are food for many desert creatures, including the spine-covered moloch lizard that lives in deserts in central Australia. Also known as the thorny devil, this creature wanders around slowly, snapping up ants, termites and other bugs on its way.

With its huge ears, the fennec fox can hear the noise of bugs running over sand.

The moloch lizard is protected by its sharp spines.

Desert food

Like many desert animals, the fennec fox of the Sahara Desert eats whatever it finds. Its favourites are bugs, birds, lizards and eggs. It will also eat fruits and berries when it finds them.

The North American kangaroo rat has large feet.

Moving in the desert

Animals that live in sandy deserts have found different ways to move around the hot, soft sand.

The marsupial mole 'swims' through the sand. It comes to the surface after rainfall.

Big feet

Since small feet sink into soft sand, many desert animals have large feet. Also, these animals usually hop rather than run. The largest feet belong to the kangaroos and wallabies that live in Australian deserts. Small creatures, such as jerboas, gerbils, jirds, kangaroo rats and hopping mice, also have big feet for their body size. They take long leaps and use their tail to keep their balance.

Wow!

Australia's marsupial mole has a pouch for its young, like a kangaroo. This pouch opens backwards, otherwise it would fill with sand while it was digging!

On hot sand, lizards lift their feet in turn to cool them.

Wriggling around

Another way that animals move about in the desert is to 'swim' through sand. The sandfish of the Arabian Desert is a lizard with small legs. It wriggles into the sand to avoid the Sun's heat and to find its **prey** of bugs and grubs.

Sidewinding snakes

Some desert snakes move with a motion called a 'sidewind'. They lift and curve their bodies sideways, leaving marks in the sand. The North American sidewinder and Namib sidewinder both do this.

A sidewinder snake forms an 'S' shape as it moves over desert sand.

The camel spider has large pincers.

The desert at night

In the desert, one way to avoid the glaring sun and scorching heat is to sleep by day and come out at night.

Listening for danger

During the day, very few animals are seen in the desert. But at night, many creatures are active. Most of these have big eyes to see in the dark, even on the blackest night. Their big ears can hear danger and their keen noses smell food or **predators**.

Food for winter

The American desert pocket mouse comes out of its burrow at night to search for seeds and bits of plants. It takes food back to its burrow to store for the winter.

Water-holding frogs sleep underground in a slimy bag.

When the Sun sets in southern Africa, the bat-eared fox comes out to hunt.

It's so... spidery!

The camel spider, which is larger than a human hand, is not a true spider. It is, in fact, an animal called a solifuge. It hunts beetles, bugs and lizards.

Hunting at night

Most owls hunt at night, so mice and similar desert creatures are always in danger. In North America, the cactus pygmy owl leaves its hole in a saguaro cactus to go hunting. The pharaoh eagle owl that lives in the Sahara and Arabian Desert is so big and powerful that it can catch and eat other owls!

Wow! In Australia, the barking owl does not hoot. Instead, it barks 'woof, woof' just like a dog!

Burrowing owls live in underground burrows in dry areas of North and South America.

Deadly desert killers

Wow!

Only two lizards are known to have poisonous bites, and both live in American deserts. They are the gila monster and the Mexican beaded lizard.

The desert is a dangerous place for small creatures. Big hunting animals, or predators, are ready to chase and kill them.

Cheetahs stalk, then chase prey.

Acrobatic hunters
In African deserts the world's fastest runner, the cheetah, races after prey such as hares and gazelles. The caracal, or desert lynx, of the same region is a smaller cat, but just as deadly. Amazingly, it can jump three metres into the air to catch flying birds.

Danger in the sky

Death can also come from the sky. In Australia, the wedge-tailed eagle soars over dry, open country looking for prey. It does not care if the animal is alive or dead! With wings that are more than two metres across, the 'wedgie' eagle is one of the world's biggest birds of prey.

Australia's big desert lizards are called goannas.

Deadly stings

Poisonous desert animals include snakes, such as the rattlesnake of North America and the desert horned viper of Africa and Arabia. There are also poisonous spiders, such as desert tarantulas, and many kinds of scorpions with deadly tail stings.

The hyena is a powerful predator that also eats any dead animals it finds.

It's so... poisonous!

Each year, more than 100,000 people are stung by scorpions, and up to 1000 die from the poison.

27

Desert oasis

Deserts are not completely dry. Sometimes, there is a pond, pool or small stream where trees grow and animals live. This is called an oasis.

Forming an oasis

How does an oasis form, especially if there is no rain? The answer is that even in a desert there can be water in rocks deep under the surface. An oasis can appear where water-bearing rocks are close to the surface. Water can be sucked up by the roots of trees and bushes such as palms, tamarugos, Joshua trees and tamarisks.

Year after year, elephants remember their long route to the Okavango Delta.

Wow!

The Okavango Delta in Africa covers about 20,000 square kilometres, the area of New Jersey in the USA or of Wales in the UK.

It's so... caring!

To fetch water, the sandgrouse flies many kilometres to an oasis, dips its sponge-like chest feathers into the water and flies back to its nest with a drink for its chicks.

A sandgrouse takes off after collecting water.

In Rajasthan's Great Indian Desert, water is scarce so people use it carefully.

Massive oasis

Animals travel long distances to drink and eat at an oasis. Elephant herds walk for many days through Africa's Kalahari Desert to reach the waters of the Okavango Delta in Botswana. This massive oasis, made up of pools and streams, is formed where the Okavango River flows into the surrounding dry land.

Tomorrow's desert

Deserts are under threat in many ways, including from people trying to grow crops and from the search for resources such as oil, metals and gems.

Pumps known as 'nodding donkeys' raise oil from deep underground in desert areas.

So much energy!

Hot deserts are good places to collect the Sun's light or heat energy as solar power to make electricity. But solar panels disturb the wildlife and can endanger many animals.

Destroying wildlife

Some desert areas, especially in the Middle East, are dotted with oil wells that bring huge wealth. People continue to drill and dig for more oil. They also search for rocks containing precious metals and minerals, such as diamonds. Some desert areas eventually turn into vast open mines, which destroys the wildlife.

Turning to dust

Not all deserts are natural. In some places, deserts form when people try to grow crops in thin soil. Often, the crops fail and the soil turns to dust and blows away. This makes 'new' desert areas that have no natural wildlife.

Visiting deserts

Deserts are now popular destinations for people to visit. But the big, noisy trucks these people sometimes use to get there can crush delicate desert plants and frighten shy animals.

Wow!

Bare rocky deserts are great places to look for animal fossils. The first fossil dinosaur eggs were found in the Gobi Desert in Mongolia.

Many people now visit the world's highest sand dunes in Namibia's Namib Desert.

Rainforests

Rain and forest

Rainforests are well named. They have lots of tall trees, close together, and it rains and rains and rains!

Warm and wet

Rainforests are wet nearly all year round. Although there may be a short dry season lasting a few weeks, it rains almost every day, week after week. **Tropical** rainforests are not only wet, they are also very warm. The temperature is at least 20°C on most days, and sometimes higher than 30°C.

Rainforest trees grow close together, forming a thick, green covering.

The rare Asiatic lion now lives only in India's Gir rainforest.

Layers of the rainforest

From the ground to the treetops, a rainforest has different layers where all sorts of animals and plants live.

Dim and quiet

If you walk though a rainforest, you notice that the forest floor is a dim and quiet place. Few flowers grow, and most animals that live here hide away. Not far above are the tops of tall bushes, shrubs and young trees. This is the **understorey layer**.

It's So... Scary!

The world's biggest spider lives on the rainforest floor in South America. The goliath tarantula is too big to sit on a dinner plate!

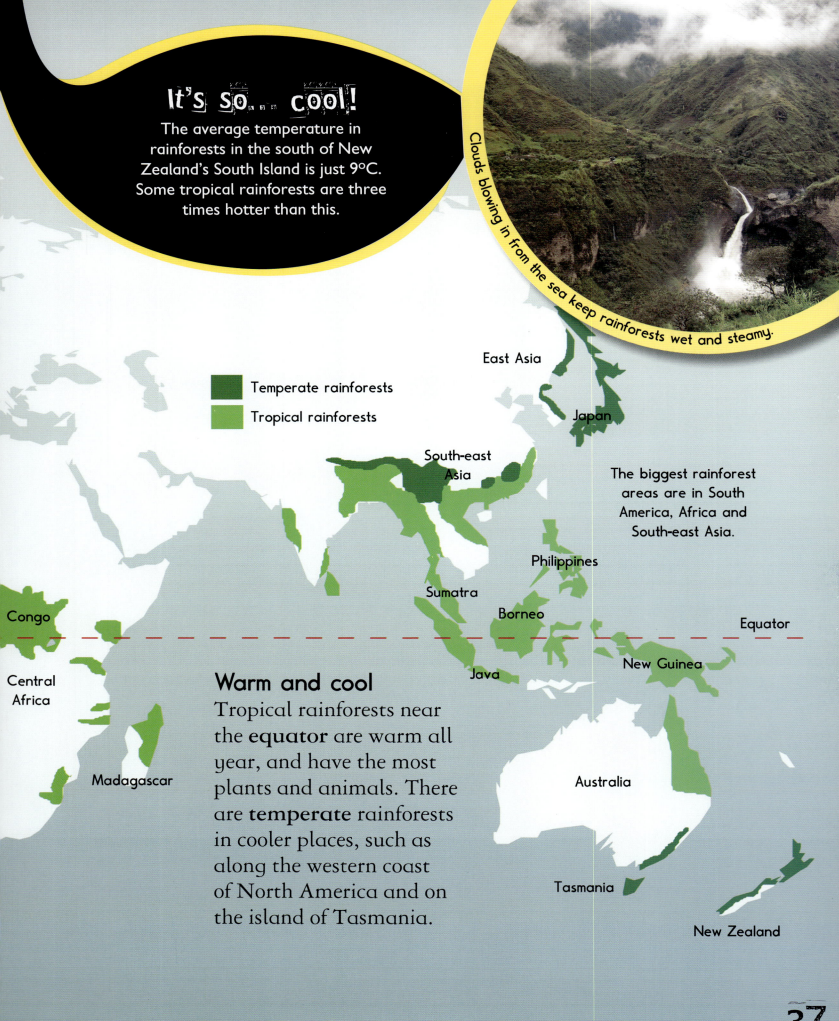

The average temperature in rainforests in the south of New Zealand's South Island is just 9°C. Some tropical rainforests are three times hotter than this.

Clouds blowing in from the sea keep rainforests wet and steamy.

East Asia

Japan

Temperate rainforests

Tropical rainforests

South-east Asia

The biggest rainforest areas are in South America, Africa and South-east Asia.

Philippines

Sumatra

Congo

Borneo

Equator

Central Africa

Java

New Guinea

Madagascar

Warm and cool

Tropical rainforests near the **equator** are warm all year, and have the most plants and animals. There are **temperate** rainforests in cooler places, such as along the western coast of North America and on the island of Tasmania.

Australia

Tasmania

New Zealand

37

Types of rainforests

Rainforests grow mainly around the middle of the world, on either side of the equator. This area is called the tropics, where it is warm all year.

North America

Central America

West Africa

Amazon

South America

Water vapour

As winds blow over oceans, they take up water. Winds do not carry water as a liquid, but as **vapour** that floats in the air and cannot be seen. The vapour makes the winds feel damp. When these winds blow over land, the water vapour changes into drops of water. These clump together to form clouds and fall as rain. Where there is most rain, rainforests grow.

Wow!

Each year, it rains on about 120 days in New York City, 180 days in London and more than 300 days in some rainforests.

Wow!

Although rainforests cover only one-sixteenth of the Earth's land area, they are home to more than half of all animals, plants and other living things.

Mangrove trees grow along some tropical coasts.

Plants and animals

Living things grow fast in a tropical rainforest's damp, steamy warmth. There are lots of amazing plants, from tiny flowers to enormous trees. Animals of every kind also live here, including worms and bugs, colourful frogs, screeching birds, huge elephants, leaping monkeys and shy gorillas.

It's so... wet!

Some rainforests get more than five times the rain in New York City, eight times more rain than London and fifteen times more than Los Angeles.

Rainforest people get food from plants in the forest.

Wow!

The strangler fig (left) is a killer! This climbing plant grows up a tree trunk, forms a tube around it and slowly kills the tree.

Busy and noisy

If you climbed right to the top of a fully grown tree in a rainforest, you would be in the **canopy layer**. This is a tangle of branches, twigs, leaves, flowers and fruits. It is a busy and noisy place, as most rainforest animals live here. Look further up, and you may see taller trees. These form the **emergent layer**, where monkeys and eagles look across the rainforest.

Emergent layer

Canopy layer

Understorey layer

Forest floor

Rainforest animals

Rainforests are full of creatures, many of which hide away quietly and are difficult to find.

Slimy trails

Rainforests are home to many types of animals. Most common are small insects, such as flies, ants and termites. Brightly coloured butterflies fly between flowers, and snails and slugs leave slimy trails.

Spider monkeys feast on fruits and flowers.

Swinging monkeys

The agile spider monkey, which lives in South American rainforests, swings from tree to tree using its hands, feet and tail to grab and hold branches. Below, fish and turtles swim in pools and swamps.

It's so... huge!

The world's biggest snakes live in rainforests. In Africa and Asia, enormous pythons swallow **prey** that is sometimes the size of a pig!

The jaguar's spotted coat helps it hide in the shadows of the forest.

Toucans crack nuts with their huge bill.

Wow!

The biggest tree-dwelling animal is the orang-utan of South-east Asia. A fully grown male can weigh 80kg, as much as a person.

Screeching toucans

Rainforests are also home to cats of all sizes. The marbled cat of Asia looks like a tiny leopard, while the jaguar of South America is almost as big as a lion. In the trees, parrots, macaws and toucans screech and flap between the branches.

Male crickets chirp to attract females.

Sounds of the rainforest

The rainforest can be one of the noisiest places in the natural world, especially at dawn and dusk.

Howler monkeys roar to protect their territory.

Day and night

Sometimes the rainforest is quiet. In the middle of the day, and for most of the night, many animals rest. At dawn and dusk, it is very different. Gibbons whoop, monkeys holler, birds chirrup, frogs croak, crickets and cicadas chirp and flies and bees buzz.

Hyacinth macaws squawk warnings to other members of their flock.

The loudest animal for its size is an insect called the cicada. If it was as big as a person, its chirps could be heard 20km away!

Wow!

It's so... loud!

The world's loudest land animals are South American howler monkeys. Their whoops carry for five kilometres through the treetops.

Attracting partners

Many of the larger creatures make sounds to defend their **territory**. This is the area of forest where they live and feed. Their calls warn others to stay away. Animals, such as frogs, crickets and birds, make special songs and sounds at breeding time to attract partners.

Colugos use skin flaps to glide from tree to tree.

Moving through the trees

Most rainforest animals live in the branches of the rainforest canopy. They have different ways of moving around the trees.

Twisting and turning

Flying is a great way to travel through, and over, the rainforest. Eagles soar above the canopy looking for prey, such as monkeys and sloths. Hawks twist and turn among the branches to grab smaller birds. At night, bats snap up insects and owls swoop down on mice and lizards.

Some flying lizards can glide up to 100 metres, using their tail to steer.

Fastest mover

One of the fastest rainforest movers is the gibbon. It swings from tree to tree using its long, powerful arms, hanging by its hook-like hands.

Gliding around

Some rainforest animals that seem to fly are really gliding through the air. Flying lizards, flying squirrels, flying frogs and flying snakes all use large flaps of parachute-like body skin to glide around.

Gibbons have curved hands and feet to grip branches.

It's so small!

The world's smallest mammal is the bumblebee bat of South-east Asia. With a body as small as a bumblebee, this tiny bat weighs less than a British 1p coin.

Wow!

The best glider is the flying lemur, or colugo, of South-east Asia. It is not a true flier, nor a lemur. But it can glide for more than 150 metres.

45

Deadly killers

Rainforest creatures are always on the lookout for danger. There could be a killer on the next branch!

Deadly poisons

Not all killers are big. Many rainforest spiders, centipedes and scorpions use poisonous bites or stings to kill their prey. Some tiny South American frogs have deadly poisons in their skin, and bright colours to warn other creatures not to eat them! Local people tip their blowdarts, arrows and spears with this poison.

The poison from one bite of a king cobra can kill an elephant.

Tiny poison arrow frogs are only as long as your thumb.

Wow!

The poison in the skin of one poison arrow frog is so powerful it could kill up to 20 people!

Large predators

Some of the world's most powerful **predators** live in rainforests. The largest big cat is the tiger, which stalks Asian rainforests for deer and wild pigs. In South America, the caiman lurks near swamps and snaps up turtles and fish. Growing to about 250kg, the same weight as four people, the Amazon's green anaconda is the world's heaviest snake.

Tigers are the largest hunters in the rainforest.

Caimans catch fish, turtles and crabs.

It's so poisonous!

The king cobra of Asia is the world's longest poisonous snake. It grows to be more than five metres long, and its favourite food is other snakes!

Rainforest trees

Some of the world's tallest, heaviest and fastest-growing trees are found in rainforests.

Life in a tree

Thousands of creatures depend on a rainforest tree. Caterpillars munch its leaves, hummingbirds sip nectar from its flowers, monkeys eat its fruits and birds nest in holes in its trunk. There are teak trees in Asia, mahogany trees in Africa and Central America and rosewood trees around the world. The kapok tree of Central and South America grows to be 70 metres tall. That is the same height as an 18-storey building.

Emerald tree boas snakes wrap themselves around branches and wait for prey.

Insects slip into a pitcher plant and are digested.

Using camouflage

Some animals depend so much on trees, they look like them! Stick insects, or 'walking sticks', resemble twigs. Leaf insects and the tree boa snake are green, just like leaves. The colourful flower mantis is disguised as a flower. Looking like part of the surroundings to avoid being seen is called **camouflage**.

Rosewood trees are under threat from loggers who cut them for their sweet-smelling wood.

Wow!

A few rainforest flowers grow high above the forest floor, sometimes 50 metres up in the forks of great trees.

Cooktown orchids grow in rainforests in north-eastern Australia.

The teeming canopy

In the rainforest canopy, twigs, stems, buds, blossom, fruits and seeds provide food for a huge variety of animals.

Bird life

Colourful small birds, such as sunbirds, honeyeaters and motmots, fly among branches in the rainforest. The great hornbill of South Asia has a wingspan of 1.6 metres and a huge **casque** on its head. The world's biggest eagles, the harpy eagle of Central and South America and the Philippine eagle, prey on monkeys, sloths, snakes and birds.

The great hornbill digs out insects from trees with its powerful beak.

Morpho butterflies find sunny clearings to warm themselves.

A sloth produces droppings only about once each week!

Pygmy marmosets live on the sap of rainforest trees.

Sloths sleep for 16 hours each day.

Hanging around

Some animals that live in the canopy never come down to the ground. These include monkeys, tree rats and lizards, such as iguanas and geckos. One of the slowest creatures in the canopy is the sloth. This leaf eater hangs from branches by its long curved claws, sometimes spending an entire week feeding on one tree.

It's so... little!

Marmosets are little South American rainforest monkeys. The smallest is the pygmy marmoset, with a head and body as small as a human fist.

The rafflesia plant has no leaves.

The forest floor

Some of the world's biggest and most exciting animals slip through the shadows of the rainforest floor.

Forest elephants live in small groups.

The forest okapi is a relative of the giraffe.

Moving silently

Elephants may seem easy to spot but, in West Africa, forest elephants move almost silently among the trees, hardly noticed in the gloom. Lowland gorillas, the world's biggest apes, also live here. These gentle creatures eat leaves and fruits. Tapirs are pig-like animals with a long, bendy nose. They live in South American and Asian rainforests.

The tapir's fleshy nose helps it to grab soft, tasty leaves.

Wow!

South American rainforests are home to the capybara, a huge cousin of the guinea pig. Weighing more than 60kg, it is the world's largest rodent.

Darkness below

The floor of the rainforest gets little light because of the thick canopy high above. Few small plants are able to survive on the ground. Only when a huge tree has fallen down will sunlight break through. Then the seeds of flowers, bushes and trees can grow.

It's so... smelly!

At one metre wide, the rafflesia of South-east Asia is the world's largest flower. It attracts flies to carry its **pollen** by smelling of rotting meat!

Mountain forests

Not all rainforests are found on flat lowlands. Some have developed on the sides of steep hills and mountains.

Furry gorillas

Tropical mountain rainforests grow high up. In these regions, it is not only very wet, but also cooler than in tropical lowlands. Here, animals have thick fur to keep warm. The furry mountain gorillas that live in Central Africa sleep in trees at night. Mother gorillas bend branches together to make a nest for themselves and their babies. Big male gorillas, which can weigh more than 200 kilograms, sleep in grassy nests on the ground.

A big male gorilla, or silverback, will protect his family group.

It's so... rare!

With just a few hundred left, the mountain gorilla is one of the world's rarest big animals.

54

Bamboo eater

The spectacled bear of South America lives in rainforests that are 2500 metres high in the Andes mountains. This bear eats almost any food, plant or animal. The giant panda from the cool, damp, cloudy hills of south-east China, however, prefers to eat just one kind of food. It rarely eats anything other than bamboo.

Spectacled bears can sniff out food hidden in the canopy.

Wow!

A fully grown giant panda is bigger than a person. A newborn giant panda, however, is tiny. It weighs about 100 grams, less than an apple.

Pandas have strong teeth to bite through bamboo.

55

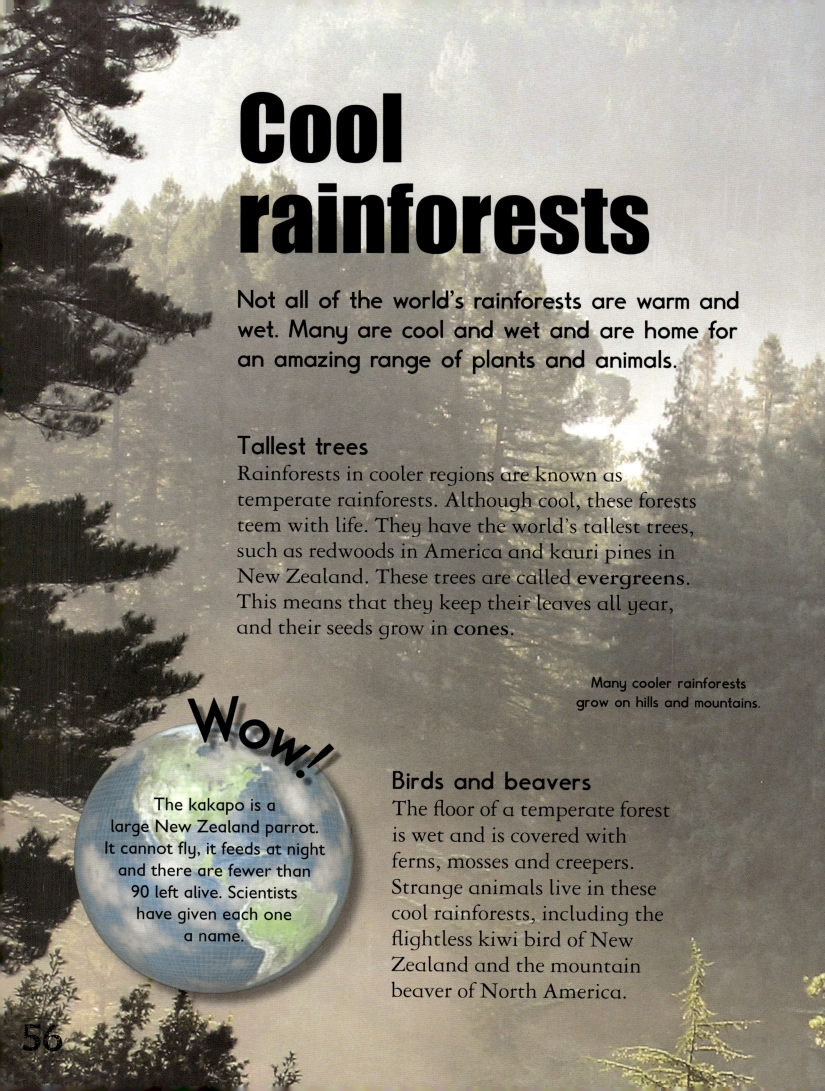

Cool rainforests

Not all of the world's rainforests are warm and wet. Many are cool and wet and are home for an amazing range of plants and animals.

Tallest trees

Rainforests in cooler regions are known as temperate rainforests. Although cool, these forests teem with life. They have the world's tallest trees, such as redwoods in America and kauri pines in New Zealand. These trees are called **evergreens**. This means that they keep their leaves all year, and their seeds grow in **cones**.

Many cooler rainforests grow on hills and mountains.

Wow!

The kakapo is a large New Zealand parrot. It cannot fly, it feeds at night and there are fewer than 90 left alive. Scientists have given each one a name.

Birds and beavers

The floor of a temperate forest is wet and is covered with ferns, mosses and creepers. Strange animals live in these cool rainforests, including the flightless kiwi bird of New Zealand and the mountain beaver of North America.

It's so... tall!

Cool rainforests have some of the tallest trees in the world. North American redwoods, Tasmanian giant gum trees and New Zealand kahikateas, or white pines, reach more than 70 metres in height.

The Tasmanian devil hunts for food at dusk in the rainforest.

The blue duiker is only 30cm tall, the height of a small dog.

Powerful bite

The blue duiker is a small, shy antelope that lives in the cool forests of central and southern Africa. The stocky Tasmanian devil is an aggressive and noisy forest creature that has one of the most powerful bites of all mammals.

Disappearing rainforests

Rainforests are the richest places in the world for wildlife. But they are also places that are most at risk, and are disappearing fast.

Laws against illegal logging are often ignored.

Destroying trees

Rainforests face many dangers, especially in the tropics. Here, trees are cut down for their strong timber, which is known as hardwood. With no trees left, many forest animals then have no homes. With no tree roots, forest soil gets washed away by heavy rain and blocks nearby rivers.

Cleared for crops

Rainforests are being cleared by fire to grow farm crops, such as sugar cane and oil palm trees. Many areas are also being planted with grass to feed cows and other **livestock**. Some rainforest animals are in danger because they are hunted for their meat.

Once the forest has been cleared, the land is used to grow crops.

Saving rainforests

All kinds of rainforest animals are at great risk, from butterflies and beetles to tigers, gorillas and rhinos. We must work hard to save rainforests, with their wonderful plants and amazing creatures.

WOW!
An area of rainforest the size of a soccer pitch is cut down every second.

The Javan rhino is almost extinct in the wild.

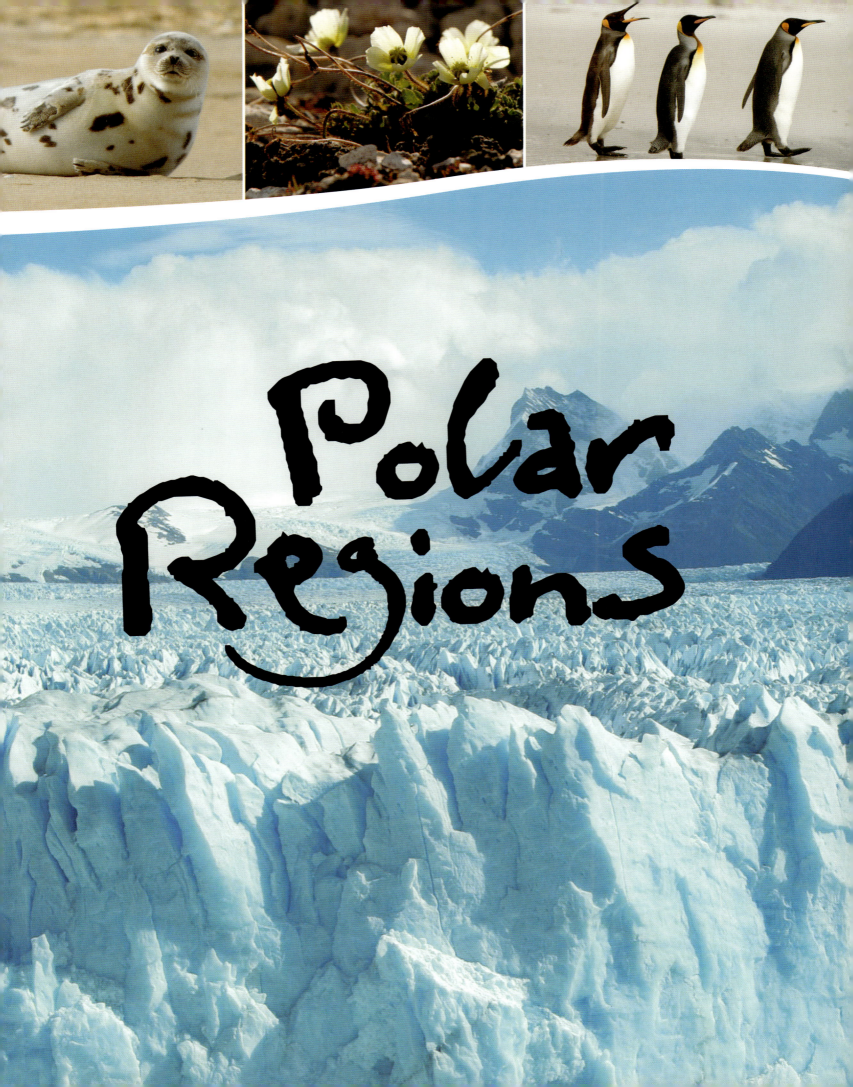

Polar Regions

Top and bottom

At the top of the world is the North Pole, and at the bottom is the South Pole. These places are cold in summer and very, very cold in winter.

Summer and winter

On Earth, the furthest points in the north and south are called the poles. The Arctic is in the far north, around the North Pole, and the Antarctic is in the far south, around the South Pole. These areas are very cold and are mainly covered in ice. Even though the sun never sets in summer, it remains cold because the sun's rays are low in the sky and weak. In winter, the sun never rises and it is freezing cold.

Polar bears live in the Arctic region around the North Pole.

North Pole

South Pole

The Earth's poles lie at opposite ends of the world and appear icy white when seen from space.

Wow!

At the North Pole, the sun rises around 21 March and does not set again for six months. At the South Pole, the sun does not rise for six months from 21 March.

It's so... c-c-cold!

The coldest temperature recorded, minus 89°C, was in the Antarctic. That is four times colder than a household freezer!

Traditionally, Inuit people of the far north catch fish through ice holes.

Life in the cold

Even in these harsh places, there is life. Fish, seals, penguins and whales swim in the seas. Small plants, such as mosses and herbs, grow in the Arctic. People live here, too.

Arctic Ocean

NORTH AMERICA

EUROPE

ASIA

AFRICA

SOUTH AMERICA

OCEANIA

Antarctic

63

The Arctic: frozen ocean

There is no land at the North Pole, not even within many hundreds of kilometres around the Pole. Much of the Arctic is a cold, shallow ocean. This is covered with ice during the long winter.

Polar aircraft have skis to land on ice and snow.

Smallest ocean

The Arctic Ocean is the world's smallest and shallowest ocean. Its average depth is only 1000 metres. It is almost entirely surrounded by land, mainly the northern parts of North America, Europe and Asia. A few seas join the Arctic Ocean, including the Laptev Sea, Kara Sea, Barents Sea and Beaufort Sea.

Not all Arctic ice is solid. In summer, some of the ice cracks into thin, floating plates called floes.

Ice sheets

In winter, more than half of the Arctic Ocean is covered by a vast, floating sheet of ice, 2 to 3 metres thick. In summer, some of the ice cracks and melts, forming jumbled blocks of ice. These lumps make travel across the Arctic's ice sheets very difficult.

Wow!

At 14 million square kilometres, the Arctic Ocean is 13 times smaller than the largest ocean, the Pacific Ocean.

It's so... far!

Many explorers have tried to march across the floating ice to the North Pole, but failed. American Robert Peary and his team said they reached the North Pole in 1909, but some experts do not agree with this.

Winter ice extent

North America
Asia
North Pole
Greenland

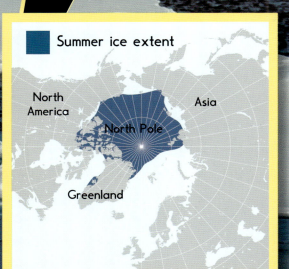

Summer ice extent

North America
Asia
North Pole
Greenland

The Arctic ice sheet is twice as large in winter compared to summer.

The grey wolf has a thick coat to keep it warm.

Northern forests

About 2500 kilometres from the North Pole are the northern lands of North America, Europe and Asia. The vast forests in these regions are some of the largest in the world.

Tough conifers

The forests of the far north are called boreal forests, or taiga. The trees here are mainly **conifers**, including pines, firs, spruces and larches. These produce their seeds in woody **cones**. Most are **evergreen**, with leaves all year round. To survive frost and snow during the long, cold winter, the leaves of these hardy trees are formed into thin needles or hard scales.

The caribou, also called the reindeer, is only found in northern regions.

The rippling Northern Lights are seen in skies around the North Pole.

WOW!

The brown bear, or grizzly, is the world's largest land meat eater. It can weigh 800 to 1000 kilograms.

Northern forests are covered in snow during the winter months.

Forest animals

Plant-eating animals of the northern forests include the snowshoe hare, the caribou and the elk, as well as birds, such as the grouse and the crossbill. These are hunted by wolves, lynxes and brown bears.

It's so... beautiful!

At night, the northern skies are sometimes lit by coloured, wavy glows called the Northern Lights, or *Aurora Borealis*.

Musk oxen grow a thick, warm fleece in winter.

In winter, the ptarmigan's white feathers help it to hide in the snow.

Treeless tundra

Between the northern forests and the shores of the Arctic Ocean to the north are tundra lands. There are no trees and they are covered in snow in winter.

It's so... frozen!

In many tundra areas, soil that is several centimetres below the surface stays frozen all year. This is called **permafrost**. It stops water draining away, which is why tundra has so many boggy pools.

Small plants and shrubs

The tundra is far too cold for trees to survive. Only small plants grow here, including mosses, lichens, tough grasses and herbs. Low-growing shrubs, such as arctic willow and birch, are also found. During the short summer, these plants provide food for animals, such as lemmings, musk oxen and ptarmigans.

Wow!

The musk ox has the longest fur of any animal. Some hairs are more than one metre in length!

The Sami people of northern Finland follow the caribou when it migrates.

Forest and tundra

In summer, caribou travel, or **migrate**, north onto the tundra to feed on the limited plant growth. In autumn, they migrate back south to the shelter of the forests. Other creatures, such as musk oxen and the Arctic fox, can stay on the tundra all year around.

Arctic poppies bloom in the short summer.

Icy shores

The shores of the Arctic Ocean are partly frozen during the long winter, although the ice melts in summer. These shores are home to many animals, including the polar bear.

Seals and walruses

Few plants grow along the shores of the Arctic Ocean. In the water, however, there is plenty of food, including fish and shellfish. These are eaten by large hunters, such as seals and long-tusked walruses.

It's so... white!

The largest polar bear stood more than 3 metres tall and weighed more than ten adult people!

Wow!

Many Arctic animals, such as polar bears, snowy owls and Arctic foxes, are white so that they blend in with the ice and snow. This is called **camouflage**.

Walruses spend most of the year in the Arctic.

Polar bears

The largest predator along the Arctic shores is the polar bear. Although it mainly eats seals, the polar bear also feeds on seabirds, fish and even small whales. When it cannot find animals to eat, the polar bear will eat berries, mosses and other plants.

A mother polar bear teaches her young how to hunt.

Each year, guillemots fly to the Arctic to breed.

The Arctic fox has the warmest fur of any mammal.

71

Seas of the north

The Arctic Ocean is extremely cold, but contains plenty to eat. The small sea animals that live here are food for larger creatures, such as great whales and killer whales.

A mother harp seal returns from hunting to feed her pup.

Tiny floating plants

The Arctic Ocean is home to many kinds of seal and whale. Beluga and killer whales live here alongside larger whales, such as the northern right whale and the bowhead whale. These large sea **predators** feed on smaller creatures, which eat even smaller ones. These then feed on tiny plants called **phytoplankton**, which grow during the long hours of summer daylight.

Wow!

The bowhead whale has the largest mouth of any animal. Its mouth is up to 4 metres long – a quarter of its body length.

Thick blubber

Many sea animals need protection against the bitter cold of the Arctic Ocean. Whales, seals and walruses have a thick layer of fat under the skin, called blubber, to keep in body warmth.

Male narwhals display their tusk at breeding time.

The beluga, or white whale, grows up to 5 metres in length.

It's so... sharp!

The narwhal whale stays in Arctic waters all year. The male's upper tooth grows into a long, sharp tusk that is used for fighting during the breeding season.

Visitors to the north

In summer, plants grow quickly in the Arctic. They provide food for animals that arrive each year for a few months.

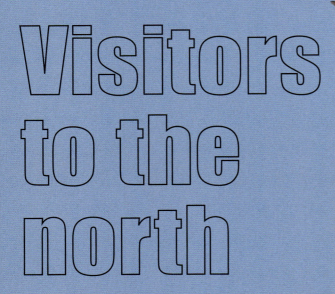

Arctic terns snatch fish from just below the surface of the water.

Snow geese remember their migration route year after year.

Arctic migrants

Animals that make long journeys each year are called migrants. Many Arctic migrants are birds, such as terns, geese and ducks. They fly north in spring to nest on the tundra, feed on plants and small creatures, and raise their chicks. When the days get shorter in the cold autumn, they fly back south to warmer lands.

Wow!

The Arctic tern spends one summer in the Arctic, before flying south for another summer in the Antarctic — a yearly journey of 35,000 kilometres.

Warmer waters

Sea animals that migrate to the Arctic for summer include blue whales, sperm whales and sea lions. Grey whales swim up the Pacific coast of North America in spring to feed near Alaska and in the Bering Sea. In autumn, they return south to have their babies in warmer waters.

The grey whale has small creatures called barnacles living on its head.

It's so... long distance!

Grey whales make the longest migration of any mammal — a yearly trip of up to 20,000 kilometres.

The Antarctic: frozen land

Antarctica is at the opposite end of the world to the Arctic. It is a frozen land surrounded by ocean – the Arctic is a frozen ocean surrounded by land.

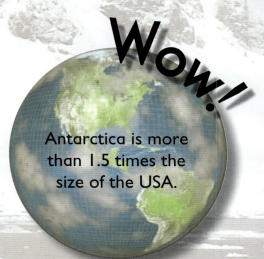

Wow!

Antarctica is more than 1.5 times the size of the USA.

Hidden mountains

Antarctica is a vast **landmass**, making up one-tenth of the world's land area. It is nearly all covered by a giant ice cap, which is an average of 2000 metres thick, although in some places it is up to 4500 metres thick. Under the ice are mountains, valleys and lakes.

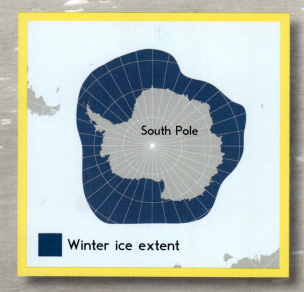

South Pole

Winter ice extent

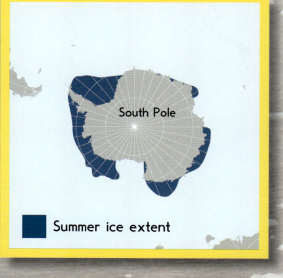

South Pole

Summer ice extent

The Antarctic sea ice sheet spreads during the freezing winter months.

Cold, windy and dry

Antarctica is not only the coldest place on Earth, it is also the windiest. Its gale-force storms can last for weeks. It is also a desert. At the South Pole, near the middle of Antarctica, the snowfall is equal to just 2.5 centimetres of rain each year. This is not much more than the rainfall in parts of the Sahara Desert.

On 14 December 1911, Norwegian Roald Amundsen and his team were the first to reach the South Pole.

Antarctica's coast has steep cliffs and icy seas.

It's so hidden!

Lake Vostok in the Antarctic is buried under 4 kilometres of ice and has not been visible for 40 million years.

King penguins rest on ice before diving into the cold water to hunt for fish.

77

Southern Ocean

Around Antarctica is the great Southern Ocean. It is 1.5 times bigger and much deeper than the Arctic Ocean. It teems with life in the summer months.

The Antarctic fin whale is 22 metres long and weighs up to 70 tonnes.

Wow!!

Each day, a blue whale can eat more than four million shrimplike krill!

Food chain

The Southern Ocean, like the Arctic Ocean, is cold but rich in nutrients. During the summer months, when there is plenty of light, tiny phytoplankton grow. These are eaten by tiny **zooplankton**, which are in turn food for bigger creatures, such as fish and squid.

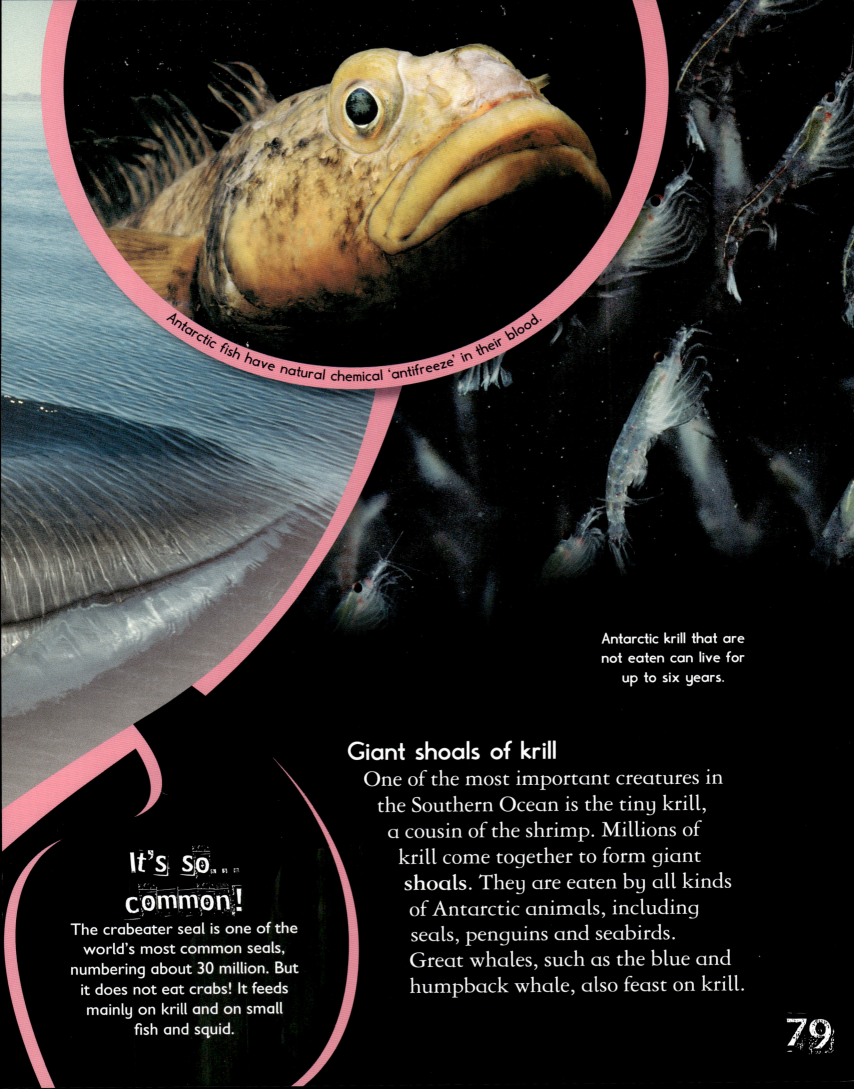

Antarctic fish have natural chemical 'antifreeze' in their blood.

Antarctic krill that are
not eaten can live for
up to six years.

Giant shoals of krill

One of the most important creatures in
the Southern Ocean is the tiny krill,
a cousin of the shrimp. Millions of
krill come together to form giant
shoals. They are eaten by all kinds
of Antarctic animals, including
seals, penguins and seabirds.
Great whales, such as the blue and
humpback whale, also feast on krill.

It's so common!

The crabeater seal is one of the
world's most common seals,
numbering about 30 million. But
it does not eat crabs! It feeds
mainly on krill and on small
fish and squid.

Islands of ice

Icebergs are massive lumps of ice that have broken off ice caps around polar lands. Antarctica has the biggest icebergs. Some are the size of small countries.

The leopard seal has sharp front teeth for feeding on prey.

Layers of ice

Over hundreds of years, the snow that has fallen on polar lands, such as Antarctica in the south and Greenland in the north, has been squashed into layers of ice. Gradually, these layers have been squeezed, causing them to slide off sideways towards the coast. At the coast, big lumps of ice break off into the ocean and drift away as icebergs.

Wow!

The enormous male southern elephant seal can weigh up to 4000 kilograms – as heavy as an elephant!

Resting and hiding

Icebergs are like floating islands, and some can last for many years before melting away. They are ideal resting places for seabirds, such as petrels and penguins, as well as seals. Icebergs also contain handy hiding places. The leopard seal lurks around the edges of icebergs, waiting to grab a penguin or small seal that passes by.

Chinstrap penguins sometimes breed on icebergs.

Only one-eighth of an iceberg is above water.

The coldest place

Nowhere on Earth is as cold as Antarctica. Around its icy coasts, the average temperature is 0°C, and that is in summer!

Winter freeze

The ice melts in summer at a few places around the edge of Antarctica. Small plants can then grow, including mosses and lichens, and little flowers, such as the Antarctic pearlwort. The tiny creatures that live in the thin soil, such as the insect-like springtail, must survive being frozen all winter.

Wow!

Male emperor penguins can survive temperatures of minus 40°C, winds of more than 200 kilometres an hour and weeks of almost constant darkness.

It's so... far!
Some emperor penguins march more than 100 kilometres from the sea to their breeding site.

Emperor penguins

Amazingly, emperor penguins can live in Antarctica through the long, bitter winters. These penguins walk from the sea to their traditional breeding sites. The female lays an egg and goes back to sea to feed. The male keeps the egg warm on his feet and huddles with other males through the freezing winter. The females return two months later to help feed their new chicks.

Snow petrels breed further south than any other bird.

Emperor penguins huddle together to protect the chicks and keep them warm.

Young king penguins chicks are kept warm by their parents.

Polar people

People have lived in the Arctic region for thousands of years. Their traditional way of life makes every use of natural resources.

Inuit people hunt and fish in boats called kayaks.

Arctic dwellers

Many groups of people, such as the Yu'pik, Chukchi, Koryak, Aleuts and Inuit, live on the lands around the Arctic. They have developed skills to find food, make shelters and survive the cold. Much of their food comes from the sea in the form of fish, seals and whales. Caribou and other animals are also part of their diet.

It's so green!

When Viking explorers arrived in Greenland 1000 years ago, the climate was warmer and there were trees, shrubs and grass. They called the region 'Greenland'. Today, it is covered in ice.

A small harpoon head carved from ivory.

Wow!

People of the far north have many words for snow. For example, *mauja* is soft, deep snow, and *pukak* is powdery, loose snow.

An igloo is a temporary shelter made from snow blocks.

Skins and bones

Arctic creatures provide much more than food. The skins of seals and caribou are used to make clothes, boots and tents. Horns, tusks and baleen, or whalebone, are carved into kitchen utensils and tools. These are also used to craft jewellery and other items.

Protect the poles

Even though polar regions are far away, they are at risk from the effects of the modern world.

Mining for minerals

About 300 years ago, people began sailing to polar seas to kill seals, whales and other animals. They also explored the land for valuable **minerals**, such as oil, coal and precious gems. Today, oil wells and mines dot the land and oil spills from huge tanker ships have ruined some areas.

Cruise ships bring tourists to see polar wildlife.

It's so safe?

The Southern Ocean is a vast **sanctuary** where whales are protected. However, ships still catch fish, squid and krill, which means whales have less to eat.

Melting ice

Polar lands and seas need protection from pollution. Dangerous chemicals are spreading in polar waters and the protective **ozone gas** high in the sky has been damaged by chemicals from aerosol spray cans and fridges. Many scientists believe that **global warming** is melting the polar ice caps, destroying the natural **habitats** of people and animals.

Wow!

If all the ice in the polar ice caps melted, sea levels would rise by more than 50 metres. This would flood many great cities along shores and coasts.

There are many oil pipelines and tankers in Alaska, USA.

Damage caused by oil spills can last many years.

Oceans

Wet world

Only 30 percent of the Earth's surface is made up of earth and rocks. The other 70 percent consists of water in rivers, lakes, seas and oceans.

Salty water

Most of the world's water is the salty water of the seas and oceans. This includes warm, shallow **bays** and colourful, **tropical reefs** as well as the huge, wide-open expanses and cold, dark depths of the oceans.

On a rescue mission, the coast guard often has to battle stormy seas.

It's so... big!

The world's largest ocean is the Pacific. It covers one-third of the world — 18 times larger than the USA and more than 700 times larger than the UK!

Tropical islands are surrounded by a vast ocean.

Wow!

The five oceans are:
Pacific (180 million km²)
Atlantic (106 million km²)
Indian (73 million km²)
Southern (20 million km²)
Arctic (14 million km²)

Mysterious oceans

Oceans are the largest areas of salty water. Seas, such as the Caribbean and Mediterranean, are smaller and are partly surrounded by land. The oceans are so vast that there is still plenty of exploring to do. Many mysteries lurk in their depths!

Marlin are among the largest, fastest fish in the world's oceans.

Arctic Ocean

Atlantic Ocean

Mediterranean Sea

Caribbean Sea

Equator

Pacific Ocean

Indian Ocean

Southern Ocean

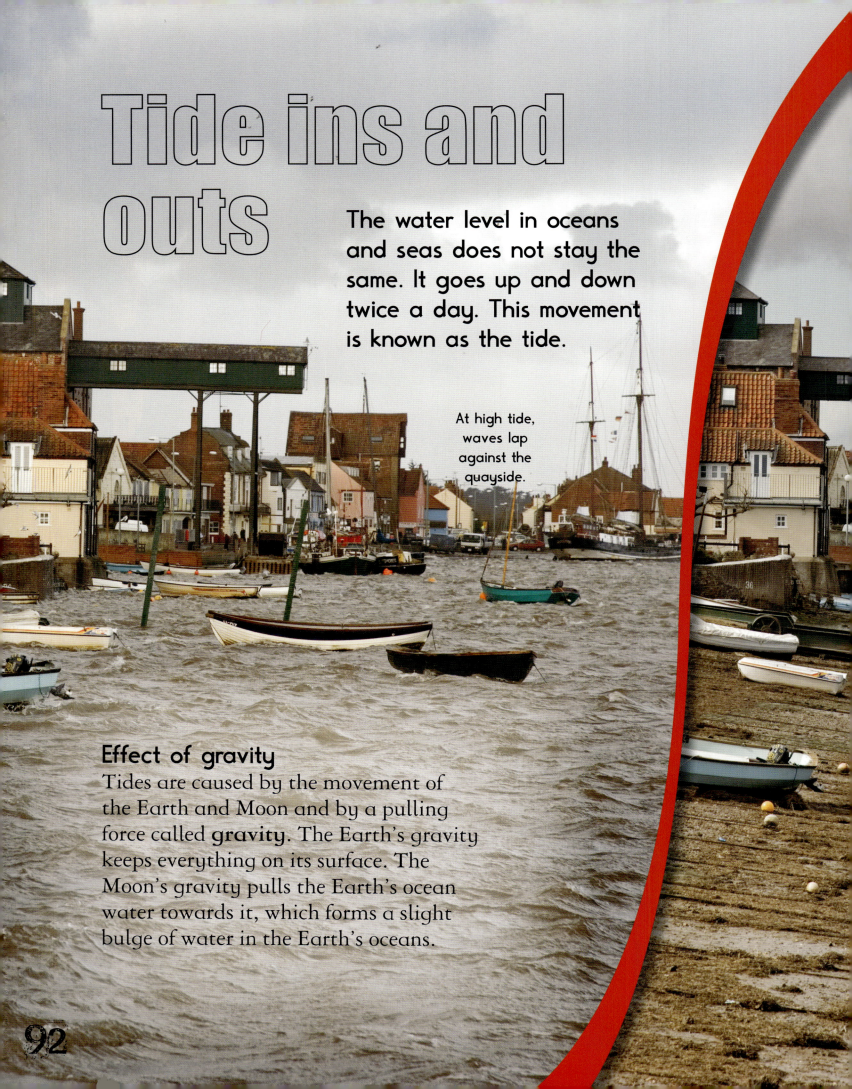

Tide ins and outs

The water level in oceans and seas does not stay the same. It goes up and down twice a day. This movement is known as the tide.

At high tide, waves lap against the quayside.

Effect of gravity

Tides are caused by the movement of the Earth and Moon and by a pulling force called **gravity**. The Earth's gravity keeps everything on its surface. The Moon's gravity pulls the Earth's ocean water towards it, which forms a slight bulge of water in the Earth's oceans.

Water levels

High tides are caused by the bulge of water in the oceans. As the Earth continues to turn, the water level goes down again. This is called **low tide**. Tides can move plants and animals along the shore, as well as ships in harbours and ports.

At low tide, small boats sit out of the water.

Wow!

Canada's Bay of Fundy has the biggest tides. The difference between high and low tide is 16 metres, the same as ten people standing on each other's heads!

Very low tides can leave ships stuck near the shore.

It's so... confusing!

Spring tides are extra-high tides that occur every two weeks, when the Sun lines up with the Moon. They do not just happen in spring!

Meet the sea

Without rivers, seas and oceans around the world would dry up. Luckily, rivers pour water into them and keep them topped up.

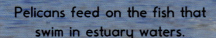

Pelicans feed on the fish that swim in estuary waters.

A saltwater crocodile warms up on a mudbank before sliding into the water.

Sand and mud

As rivers get close to the sea, they widen into a mouth called an **estuary**, or bay. Rivers carry tiny pieces of sand and mud. Near the sea, rivers slow down and the sand and mud fall to the bottom. This is why estuaries and bays often have shallow mud flats, salt marshes and sandbanks.

Wow!

About one-fifth of all the river water that flows into the world's oceans every day comes from the huge Amazon River.

In summer, flowers bloom on salt marshes.

Teeming with life

Although the surface of the mud and sand may look bare, underneath it is teeming with life. Here, creatures, such as worms, shrimps, crabs and shellfish, live in huge numbers. As the tide comes in, these animals come out to feed on tiny bits of food. But when they do this, they are in danger from hungry fish and birds.

Fiddler crabs live in salty marshes.

It's so big!

The world's biggest reptile is the estuarine crocodile, also called the saltwater crocodile. It lives around South-east Asia and Australia, and grows to be 7 metres long.

On the beach

Sea currents, waves and tides not only move sand and pebbles on a beach, they also wash up seaweed, animals and litter.

Weeverfish bury themselves in sand.

It's so... poisonous!

The weeverfish, which is found in European waters, hides in sand and has poisonous fin spines on its back.

Sea lions crowd onto beaches to rest.

Strong currents

Sand is made up of tiny bits of broken rock and animal shells. Waves and water movements, called **currents**, move this sand around. Although small waves and light currents leave the sand in place, larger waves and strong currents can wash sand away to leave larger bits called shingle.

Wading birds search for food in sand and mud.

Bits and pieces

As the tide rises and then falls, it washes up many things, including straggly seaweed, dead fish, starfish, shells and driftwood. This area is called the **strandline**. Unfortunately, you will usually also find man-made rubbish, such as plastic bottles and bags.

Baby turtles race to the sea before gulls, crabs, lizards and other animals eat them.

Wow!

Sea turtles, which are now very rare, lay eggs in beach sand. Their babies hatch out a few weeks later and run to the sea.

Cliffs and rocky shores

Where ocean waves crash against hard rocks, they form tall cliffs and rock pools below. These are home for large numbers of animals.

Tall cliffs

Although cliffs and rocky shores can be dangerous places, many creatures live here. Birds, such as gannets, razorbills and guillemots, nest on tiny ledges along steep cliffs. They fly out to sea to catch fish for their chicks.

Waves can wear rocks into amazing shapes, such as these tall sea stacks.

Cliff-nesting birds are safe from many enemies.

Rock pools

As the tide goes out, it leaves small pools among the rocks. These teem with all kinds of animals. Crabs hide under stones, and blennies, gobies and other fish take cover among slippery seaweed. Anemones sting shrimps and tiny fish with their tentacles.

Anemones look like flowers, but most are poisonous.

Wow!

In Australia, the blue-ringed octopus lives in rock pools. It is very small, but has a deadly bite. It has enough poison to kill ten people!

It's so... tall!

The tallest sea cliffs are at Kalaupapa in Hawaii. They tower 1000 metres above the sea. This is 2.5 times higher than New York's Empire State Building and three times higher than France's Eiffel Tower.

In the shallows

Around many coasts are areas of sea less than 200 metres deep. Here, rather than the deep ocean, is where most sea creatures live.

Sunlight and nutrients

Plants, such as eel grass, wracks and oarweeds, grow well in shallow waters. This is because lots of sunlight reaches the bottom and plenty of **nutrients** are deposited by rivers. These plants provide food and shelter for all kinds of small animals, such as fish, crabs, worms and shellfish.

Manatees live in shallow and warm bays, estuaries and lagoons.

Seaweeds, such as bladderwrack and hollow green-weed, form beautiful underwater gardens.

Wow!

The manatee, also called the sea cow, eats sea grass. The manatee has flippers and a round tail, and grows to be as large as a real cow!

Plaice can change colour to look like sand.

Hunting in the shallows

Larger creatures, such as octopuses, seals and porpoises, hunt among the weeds and rocks. Flatfish, such as plaice, soles and flounders, also search for **prey**. These fish lie hidden on the seafloor and wait for their prey to come near. Then they pounce.

The octopus grabs prey with eight suckered tentacles.

It's so... long!

Jellyfish are simple creatures with no skeleton, brain or heart. Some have very long stinging tentacles with which they catch fish and other prey.

Colourful corals

Coral reefs grow where the water is warm, shallow and clear. Reefs have more kinds of wildlife than any other place in the sea.

Stony cups

Coral reefs are huge rocks with lots of cracks, caves and ledges. Tiny coral animals build stony cups around themselves for protection and when they die, they leave behind the hard cups. These build up into the reef. Different kinds of corals make different shapes, including mushrooms, vases, tubes, horns and fans.

Few places are as colourful as a coral reef.

Coral creatures have stinging tentacles.

It's so... threatened!

Coral reefs face many dangers, including people collecting their corals and shells and damage caused by boats. Mud and silt deposits also kill the tiny coral animals.

Prowling the reef

Fish and shrimps swim among the coral, along with starfish, sea urchins and worms. Their bright colours make them easy to see by others of their kind. Sharks, such as the black-tipped reef shark, prowl around the reef edge, waiting to snap up prey.

Giant groupers can swallow other fish whole.

Wow!

One of the biggest reef fish is the giant grouper, which has a mouth as big as wheelie bin!

Sea horses are fish that swim slowly and suck in tiny bits of food.

Moving and breathing

Animals need to breathe oxygen to stay alive. Some sea creatures breathe air like humans, while others breathe underwater using gills.

Taking a breath

Sea animals that breathe air include whales, dolphins, seals, sea lions, turtles and sea snakes. They come to the surface now and then to take a breath. If they are unlucky enough to get trapped under the water's surface by fishing nets, they drown.

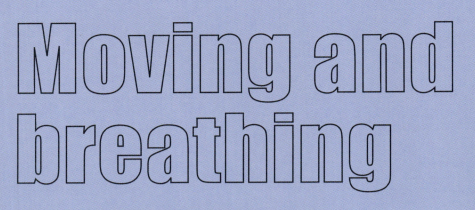

Dolphins breathe through the blowhole on top of their head.

Wow!

Some whales can hold their breath for more than two hours when they dive deep into the ocean to search for food!

Sea snakes swim by wriggling through the water.

Using gills

Fish, squid, sea worms and starfish all breathe underwater. They have frilly tissues called gills, which take in **oxygen** from the water. On most fish, the gills are found under slits on each side of the front part of their body.

Speedy squid can swim through the water quickly.

Moving around

Animals in the sea move in different ways. Fish swish their fins and tail, whales flap their flukes, or tail, and crabs run sideways. A squid pushes itself through the water by squirting water.

It's so... fast!

The oceans' fastest swimmer is the sailfish. It can swim at more than 100 kilometres an hour, almost as fast as the cheetah can run.

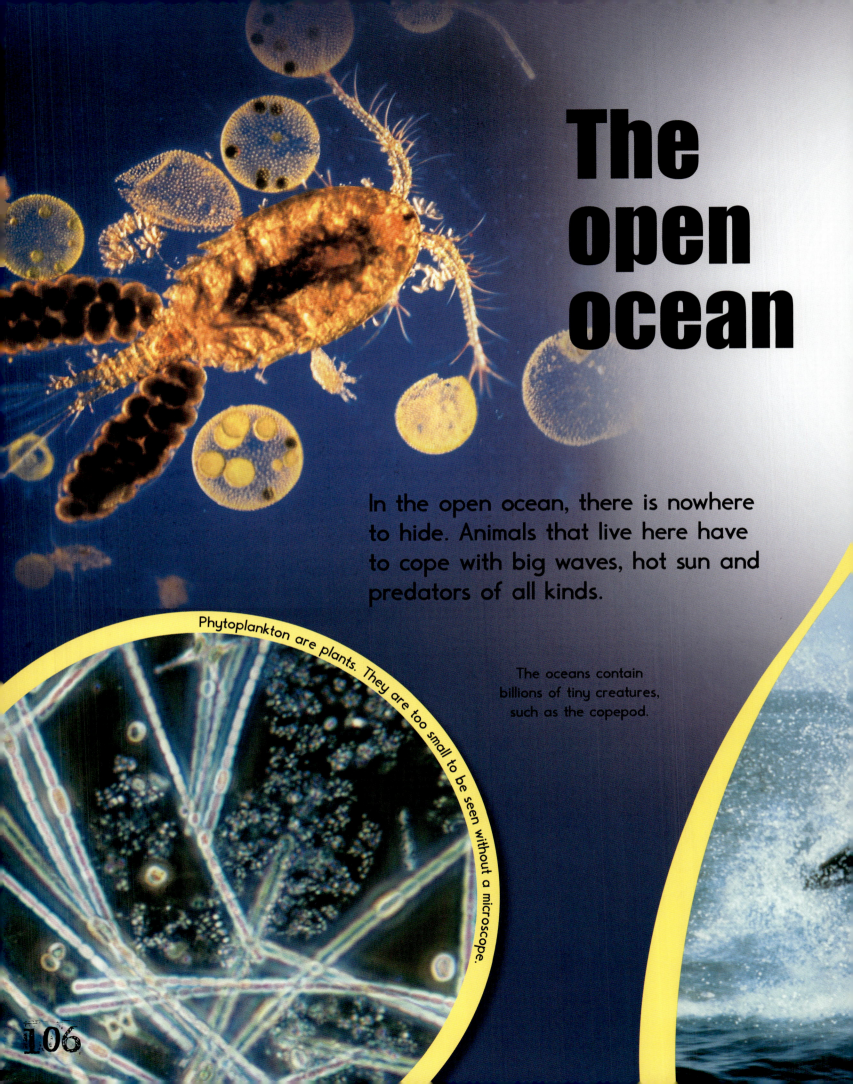

The open ocean

In the open ocean, there is nowhere to hide. Animals that live here have to cope with big waves, hot sun and predators of all kinds.

Phytoplankton are plants. They are too small to be seen without a microscope.

The oceans contain billions of tiny creatures, such as the copepod.

It's so... massive!

The largest fish is the whale shark. At 12 metres long, it is as big as a school bus. But it is not dangerous. It feeds on tiny creatures called plankton.

Killer whales hunt many creatures, including seals, fish and seabirds.

Plant plankton

There are few seaweeds in the open ocean, but there are billions of minuscule plants called **phytoplankton**. These are eaten by very small animals, who are then food for small fish, squid and other creatures. Larger fish eat these, and are in turn food for bigger creatures, right up to the largest ocean hunters such as the great white shark and killer whale.

Wow!

The world's largest hunter is the sperm whale. It grows up to 18 metres long and can weigh up to 50,000 kilograms – the same as seven African elephants!

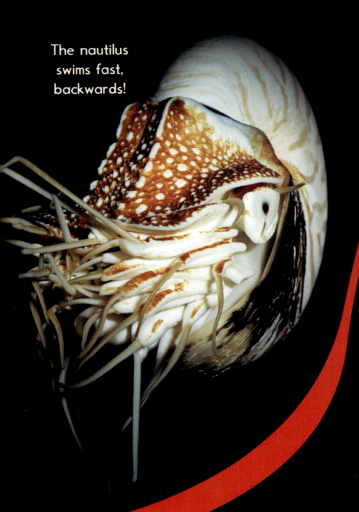

The nautilus swims fast, backwards!

Twilight zone

Far below the ocean surface is a dim and gloomy world. Here, animals have big eyes to see in the half-light of the dark depths.

Strange creatures

Deeper in the ocean there is less sunlight, so plants cannot grow. Some amazing creatures live here, including strange fish, jellyfish, worms, squid and octopuses. These animals swim or drift all their lives and never touch anything solid. They eat dead creatures that drift down from above, or hunt and eat each other.

It's so... weird!

The nautilus, a cousin of the octopus, has a stripy coiled shell. It has big eyes to see in the gloom and more than 80 tentacles to catch fish.

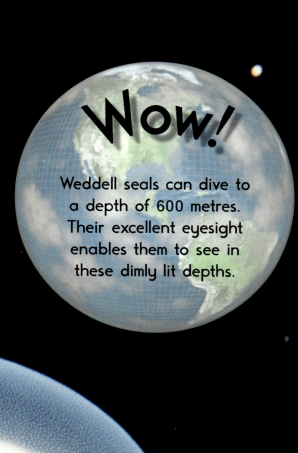

Wow!

Weddell seals can dive to a depth of 600 metres. Their excellent eyesight enables them to see in these dimly lit depths.

Flashlight fish have an area, just below each eye, that glows.

Many jellyfish produce a bright, luminous light.

Making light

Not all deep-water animals need light. Some sea animals glow in the dark! They have special body parts that make light. This is called **bioluminescence**. Flashlight fish have shining eyes, and lanternfish have spots of light along the body. There are also glowing jellyfish and squid.

Bottom of the sea

In the deepest parts of the ocean, there is no day or night, and no winter or summer. It is dark and cold all the time.

Dark region

The sun's light and warmth cannot reach deeper than 500 metres beneath the surface of the ocean. Below this, it is cold and black. This vast region is the largest place in the world. Many creatures, such as fish, squid, jellyfish and shellfish, live here.

Underwater craft, called submersibles, explore the seabed.

It's so... hot!

In some places on the seabed, boiling water spurts through vents. Here, there are giant worms as thick as your arm and as long as a car.

Wow!

The ocean's deepest place is the Mariana Trench in the north-west Pacific. It goes down 10,923 metres. Mount Everest would fit here with over 2000 metres to spare!

The anglerfish uses a glowing light to attract fish.

Ghostly fish

On the bottom of the
deep sea there are rocky
mountains, cliffs, flat plains
of mud, valleys and **canyons**.
Here live deep-sea starfish,
sea cucumbers, white crabs and pale,
ghostly fish. Many animals are blind as
there is no light, making eyes of no use.

Crabs, worms
and shellfish gather
around hot water
rising from a
deep-sea vent.

Using the oceans

Seas and oceans are very useful for people, and not just for water sports and seaside holidays.

Fishing

The world's oceans are busy with fishing boats that catch huge amounts of fish and shellfish. Seafood is especially important for people who live on small islands as it provides them with food and something to sell.

In 2004, a powerful tsunami devastated coastal regions of the Indian Ocean. Thousands of fishermen died or lost their boats and their livelihoods.

Many Asian fishermen use traps to catch fish.

A wind turbine's blades rotate to turn wind power into electricity.

Wind power

The wind out at sea is very useful to us. It whips across the oceans much faster than it does over land. A huge machine, called a turbine, turns the power of the wind into another kind of power – electricity.

Container ships carry goods in big, steel boxes.

Tsunamis cause terrible damage and loss of life.

Shipping
Oceans provide routes for the enormous ships that carry cargo from port to port. Containers on these ships are filled with all kinds of goods, from cars and shoes to toys and frozen food. Air transport is faster, but it is much cheaper to send goods by ship, and ships can carry greater weights, too.

Seas and oceans at risk

Oceans and seas are in trouble. We throw rubbish into them, pollute them with chemicals and catch too much of their wildlife.

Wow!

There are more than 170,000 different kinds, or species, of animal in the ocean. They include the world's largest animal, the blue whale.

Damaged by pollution

Seas and oceans are becoming more and more polluted. People litter the beach and dump rubbish overboard from ships and boats. Pipes from factories pour in dangerous chemicals. A giant oil tanker may have an accident and spill its thick, black oil. This floats on the sea and kills fish, seabirds and other wildlife.

Flooding lowlands

The problem of **global warming** will greatly affect seas and oceans all around the world. This warming may cause water to expand and the ice at the poles to melt. This could raise ocean levels and flood low-lying areas of land, making millions of people homeless.

Birds affected by oil spills cannot fly or catch food.

In the future, coastal flooding may well happen more often.

It's so dangerous!

Plastic bags floating in the sea look similar to jellyfish. Sea turtles eat jellyfish, but if they swallow a plastic bag by mistake, they may die.

Litter left or washed up on a beach can harm wildlife.

Glossary

Arid Extremely dry, with very little rain or other forms of moisture.

Bay Part of a coast that curves around an area of sea.

Bioluminescence When living things produce light by special chemical processes.

Camouflage Colours and patterns that blend with the surroundings, making a creature difficult to see.

Canopy layer The main level of branches, leaves and flowers in a rainforest, high above the ground.

Canyon Very deep, steep-sided valley.

Casque A helmet-like head covering.

Cone Hard, woody parts made by trees, such as pines and firs, which contain seeds.

Conifers Trees that produce their seeds in cones.

Continent A large land mass, such as Africa, North America, Antarctica and Australia.

Current Flowing movements in water.

Dusk The time around sunset, between day and night.

Emergent layer The tallest trees in a forest, above the main canopy layer.

Equator An imaginary line around the middle of the world, midway between the North Pole and South Pole.

Erosion The wearing away of soil and rocks by rain, wind and the Sun.

Estuary The end, or mouth, of a river, where it widens and flows into the sea.

Evergreen Trees that have some leaves all through the year.

Germination When a seed sends out a shoot and root and begins to grow into a plant.

Global warming Heating up of the Earth caused by changes in the gases that make up its atmosphere.

Gravity The pulling force coming from all things, especially large objects such as the Earth and Moon.

Habitats Types of places where animals and plants live, such as a wood, lake or seashore.

High tide The highest level reached by the sea. High tide happens twice a day.

Landmass A large, continuous area of land.

Livestock Animals kept by people, especially on farms, such as cows, sheep and pigs.

Low tide The lowest level of the sea. Low tide is reached twice
a day.

Migrate To make a long journey each year to a place far away, and then to return again.

Minerals A large range of natural substances that make up rocks and soil.

Native A plant, animal or person in its natural region, rather than coming from somewhere else.

Nutrients Substances used as food by living things.

Oxygen A gas that is in the air we breathe. Oxygen is also found in water and is used by underwater creatures to breathe.

Ozone gas A form of oxygen, which is high in the sky and helps protect against some of the sun's

Amundsen, sea lions 17

Permafrost Soil that stays frozen all the time, not even thawing in summer.

Phytoplankton Tiny plants, mostly too small to see, that float in seas, oceans and large lakes.

Pollen Tiny, dust-like grains that must get from the male parts of a flower to the female parts so that seeds can start to form.

Predator An animal that hunts others for food.

Prey An animal that is hunted for food.

Reef A large, rocky part of the seabed, usually built by tiny coral animals.

Sanctuary A safe, protected place.

Shoal A large gathering of water animals, such as fish or krill.

Strandline The long, thin heap of washed-up things along the shore, which is left by high tides.

Swarm A huge gathering of creatures, usually insects such as bees, wasps or locusts.

Sweat To give off moisture through the pores of the skin.

Temperate Places where it is neither very hot nor very cold, usually with warm summers and cool winters.

Territory An area where an animal lives, feeds and raises young, which it defends against others of its kind.

Tropical Around the middle of the world, in the region called the tropics, where it is very warm all year.

Tsunami A series of huge waves that is set off by underwater earthquakes.

Understorey layer Bushes, shrubs, young trees and other low-growing plants in a forest.

Urine The liquid waste produced by an animal.

Vapour In the form of a gas that floats and changes shape.

Zooplankton Tiny animals, mostly too small to see, that float in seas, oceans and large lakes.

Index